PURNELL'S LIFE CYCLE BOOK OF
frogs

Written by Ronald Ridout and Michael Holt
Illustrated by Vera Croxford

About the Authors

RONALD RIDOUT'S name appears on almost 46 million educational books. He is the "world's best selling educational writer" (*Guinness Book of Records*). A famous pioneer in the field of education, he believes that children "should get the meaning off the page".

He has published 277 books mainly educational. After gaining his diploma at Oxford University he taught for seven years, joined an educational publishing company and eventually turned to full-time writing and editing of books.

Ronald Ridout now works from his home in Haslemere and his books sell some $2\frac{1}{2}$ million copies each year.

MICHAEL HOLT has been an actor, a research physicist, an editor and a senior lecturer in mathematics.

He is now a freelance writer with a deep interest in how children learn and has written many highly successful textbooks.

Michael Holt is married with two children and lives in Herefordshire where he studies snakes, toads and frogs.

First published 1974 by Purnell Books
Text copyright © 1974 RR Productions Limited and Michael Holt
Illustrations copyright © 1974 Purnell & Sons Limited

Designed and produced for Purnell Books by Intercontinental Book Productions

Printed and bound in Edinburgh by Morrison & Gibb Limited

SBN 361 02782 6

Million years ago		
Cretaceous 136	Triceratops, Brontosaurus, Tyrannosaurus	
Jurassic 195	Iguanodon, Frog, Stegosaurus	
Triassic 225	Triadobatrachus (primitive frog), Mastodonsaurus	
Permian 280	Eryops, Dimetrodon	
Carboniferous 345	Semouria	
Devonian 395	Osteolepis, Ichthyostega	

One of the earliest amphibians was the large *Eryops* which was nearly 2 metres long. This was the forefather of the early frog.

Evolution

The earliest frog first appeared on earth about 200 million years ago and lived alongside the early reptiles. The frog as we know it today developed in the Jurassic Period when the great dinosaurs such as the Horned Triceratops and the Tyrannosaurus, seen fighting in the picture below, ruled the land.

The frog can breathe and live both on land and in water. That is, it is an amphibian. The fact that the frog can live on land and in water, has helped it survive. In fact, like the crocodile, it is one of the oldest surviving species living today.

Hochstetter's frog is a New Zealander. It is the most primitive frog as well as being rare.

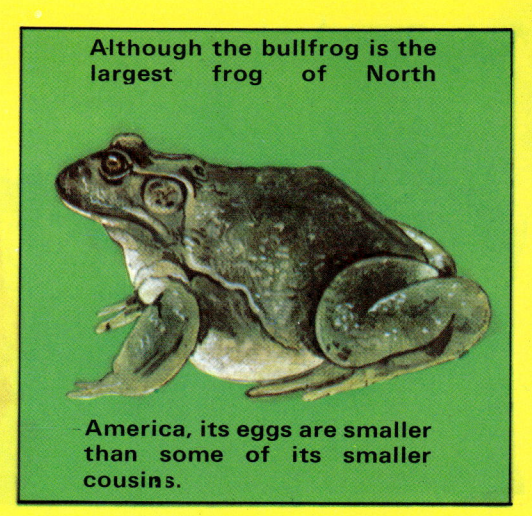

This is called the edible frog. It is eaten by man and regarded as a great delicacy.

Although the bullfrog is the largest frog of North America, its eggs are smaller than some of its smaller cousins.

Habitat

Frogs and toads live in most regions of the world. They live in both hot and temperate climates and have been able to adapt themselves to these different environments.

This is the common frog (*Rana temporia*) of Europe and Asia. The smaller black and white picture shows this frog's actual size.

A frog is a tail-less amphibian and is cold blooded. That is, it relies on the sun to warm its blood. Therefore, its body temperature is almost the same as the temperature of the surroundings.

The hedgehog is a warm-blooded animal which hibernates.

The frog in the large circle is hibernating under the damp mossy bank (small circle) and is safe from its enemy, the badger.

Hibernation

Like all other cold-blooded animals, the frog hibernates—that is, goes into a deep sleep in the winter when the sun is not strong enough to warm it sufficiently to keep it active. In the same way warm-blooded animals such as hedgehogs, bears and muskrats hibernate when there is not enough food for them to eat.

During hibernation, when the frog is sleeping, it lives off special lumps of fat called fat bodies, shown in the diagram on page 10.

Frogs hibernate in the mud at the bottom of ponds and in damp moss or holes in the ground, and their eyes, mouth and nostrils are closed.

The frog's long hind legs make it the best of leapers and an excellent swimmer. Some frogs have been known to leap 13 metres.

The leaping sequence of the frog is shown on the right.

1. The frog is in a sitting position but the muscles in its hind legs are tensed ready to push off.

2. The frog pushes itself forward and upwards until its hind legs are fully stretched.

This male edible frog has just puffed up the pea-sized sacs of skin below its ears. It has done so to make a good long sound for its mating call.

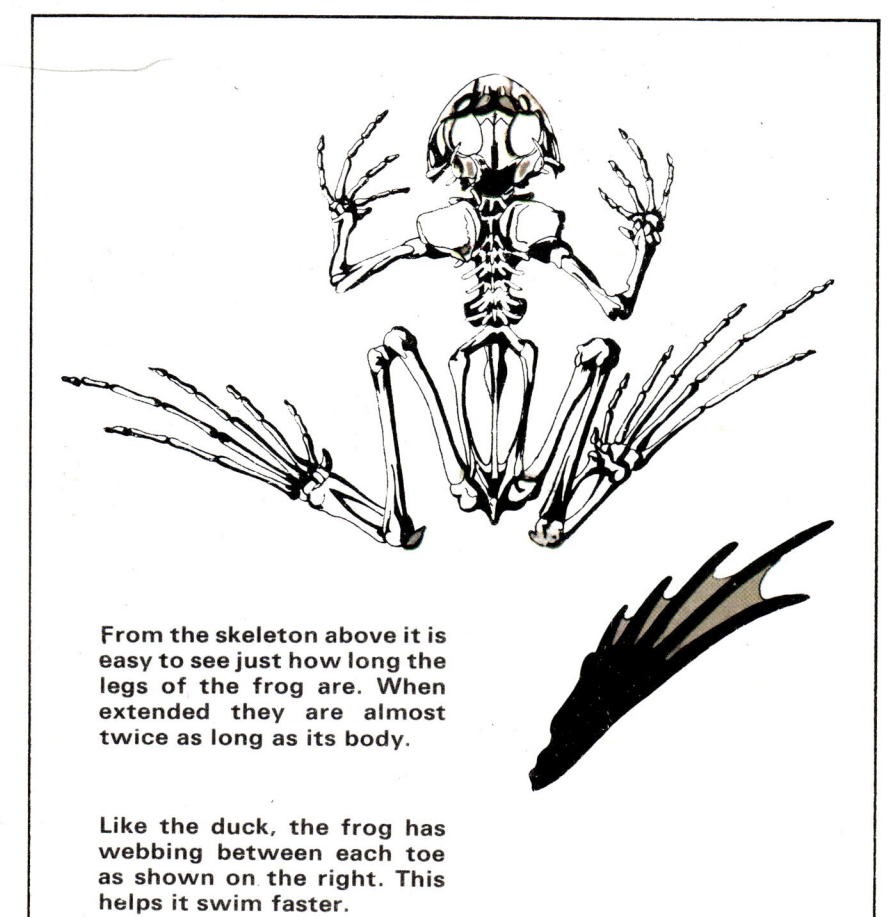

From the skeleton above it is easy to see just how long the legs of the frog are. When extended they are almost twice as long as its body.

Like the duck, the frog has webbing between each toe as shown on the right. This helps it swim faster.

After the winter sleep

In spring frogs leave their winter homes and make their way to ponds and slow-moving streams to breed. The male frogs 'sing' to the females to attract them to the breeding ponds. Their croaking is called a 'sex-call'. Some female frogs will reply to the males with a special cry of their own. When lots of frogs sing together as a 'choir', their noise can be loud enough to disturb people living near the pond.

3. The frog now draws up its hind legs and extends its forelegs ready to meet the ground.

4. The frog's front legs take up the shock of landing. The hind legs are drawn up into the body.

Reproductive organs of a female frog

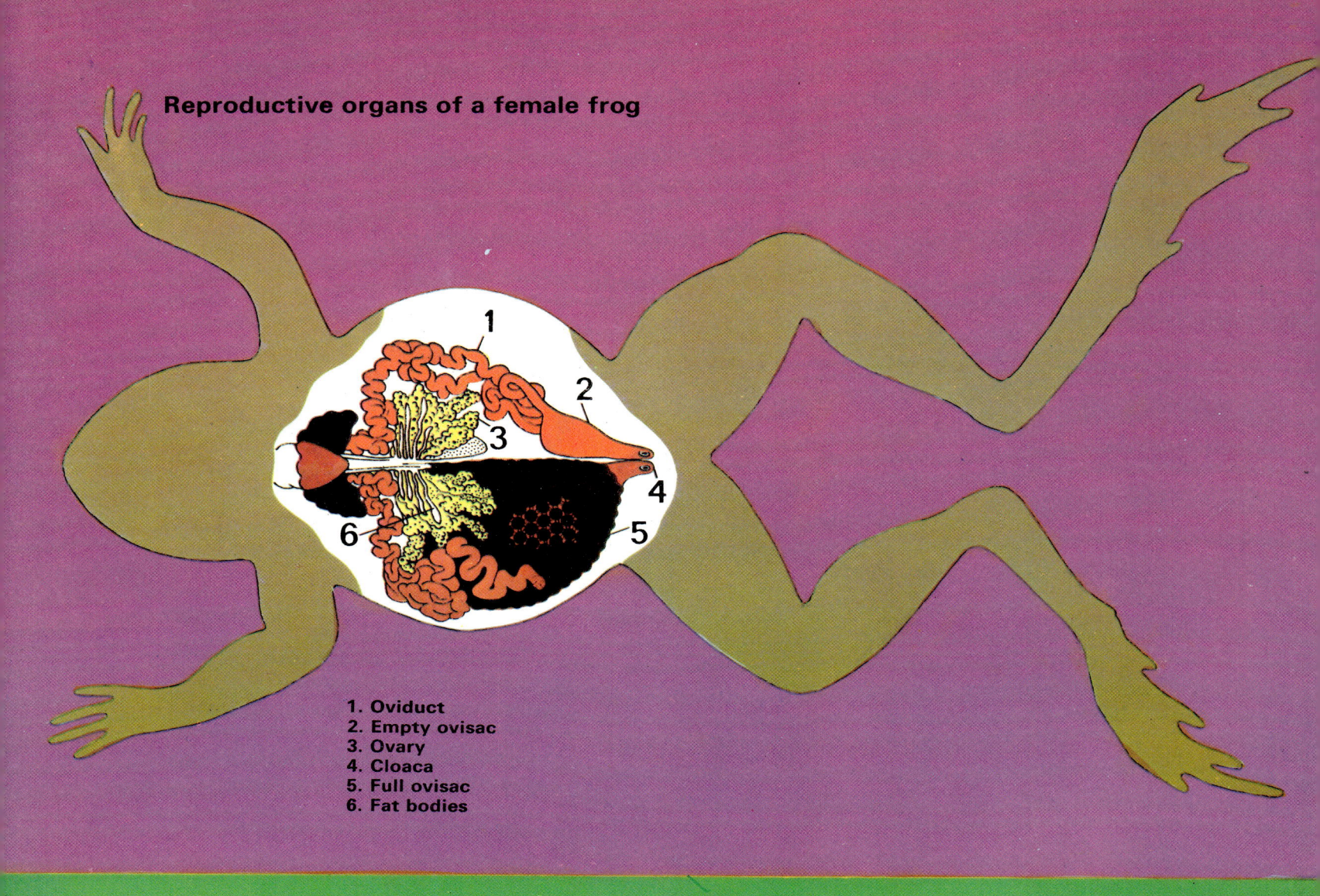

1. Oviduct
2. Empty ovisac
3. Ovary
4. Cloaca
5. Full ovisac
6. Fat bodies

Reproductive organs of a male frog

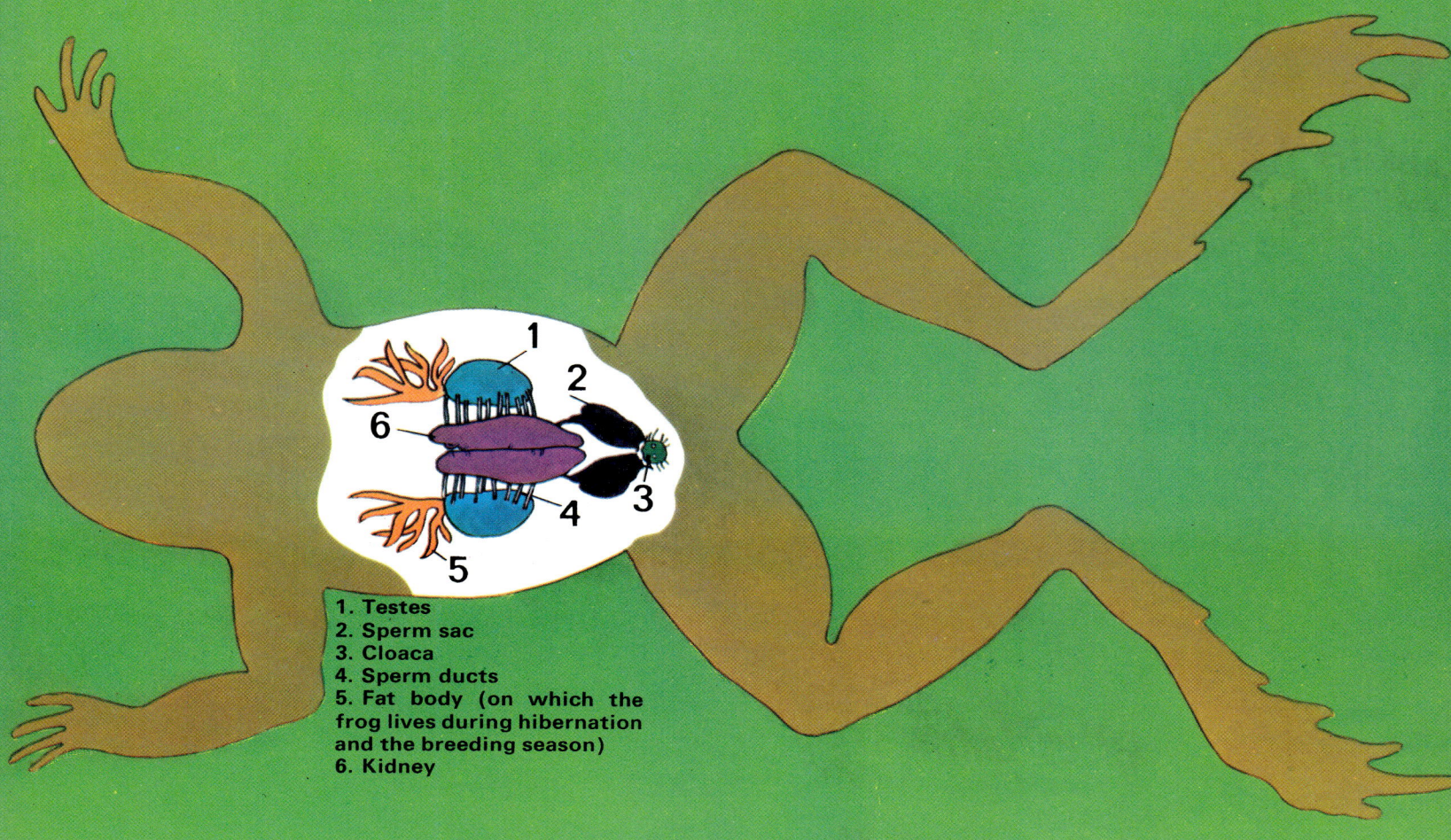

1. Testes
2. Sperm sac
3. Cloaca
4. Sperm ducts
5. Fat body (on which the frog lives during hibernation and the breeding season)
6. Kidney

The reproductive organs

The female frog makes as many as 2,000 eggs inside its body. The eggs are first made in one of its ovaries and then pass into one of the oviducts. While they are travelling through the oviduct the eggs receive their 'jelly' covering to protect them. Then they move on to the ovisac or uterus. They are stored here before being pushed out through the cloaca.

The female frog is fat and heavy while carrying its eggs. This slows it down and makes it difficult for it to escape from its enemies. The picture above shows a water-beetle about to attack a female frog. The beetle is much smaller than the frog but it will still attack the slowed-down female.

To make a frog, one egg of the female has first to be fertilised by the sperm of a male frog. The male makes millions of sperm in the testes. They pass to the kidneys through the sperm ducts into the sperm sac, where the millions of sperm are stored until they are ejected through the cloaca.

The common toad attempting to mate with a trout. If unable to free itself from the toad's firm grip, the fish will drown.

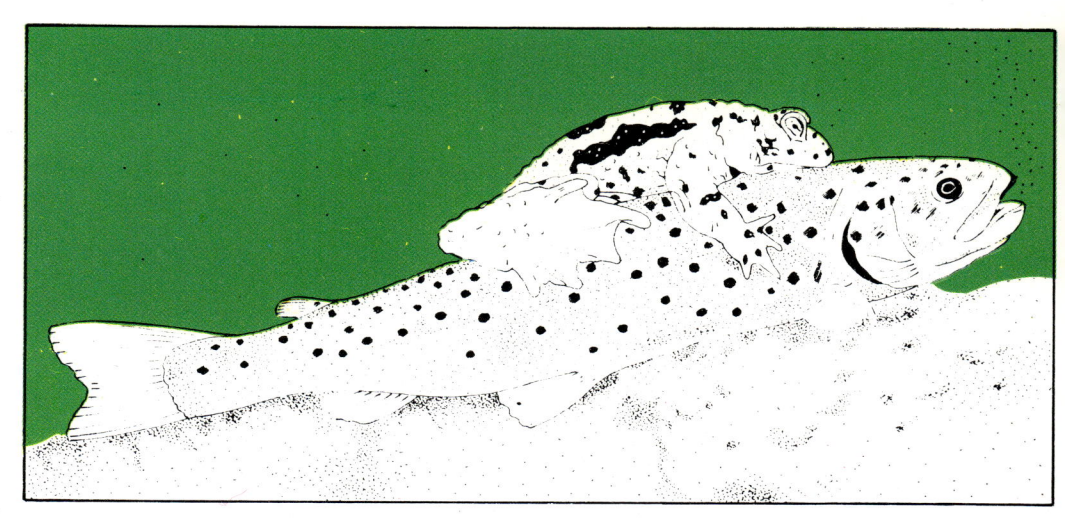

Courtship
Apart from the croaking or sex-calls, frogs do not follow a courtship pattern as many birds and animals do. But so strong is the mating instinct in male frogs and toads that if a female frog is not present, the male will attempt to mate with a fish.

Before mating with the female, the male frog grows rough black patches on its first fingers. These are called the nuptial pads and

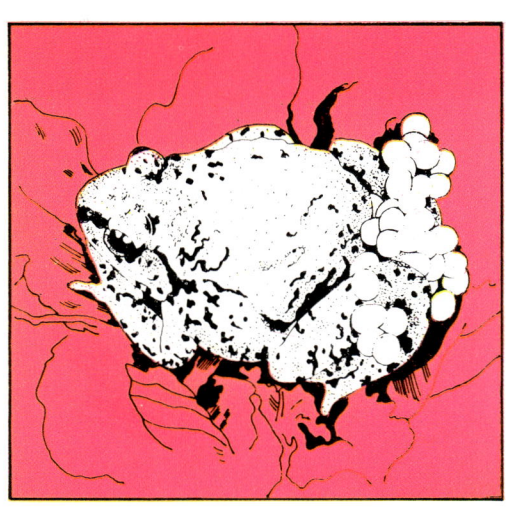

The midwife toad mates and lays its eggs on land. The male midwife toad wraps the eggs around its legs and carries them until the eggs are ready to hatch, then it returns to the water to release them.

help it grasp the skin of the female during mating. The nuptial pads can be seen in the small circular picture above. When the breeding season is over the rough patches disappear again.

To help the male recognise the female frog during the breeding season, the female's skin takes on a 'pearly' appearance and becomes rougher. She is now ready to lay her eggs in the pond's water.

The female South American marsupial frog keeps its eggs in a brood pouch on its back. Both male and female place the eggs in the pouch. When the tadpoles hatch, the female opens the pouch with a hind toe.

The male of Darwin's frog carries the eggs and tadpoles in its mouth.

Mating

The male mates with the female by climbing on to its back and gripping with the nuptial pads. The male squeezes the female's body. This releases the eggs, as the large picture above shows. Sometimes the female frog will press the eggs out through her cloaca. They will stay in this position for a day to a day and a half.

Immediately the female lays its eggs, the

Greatly magnified view of sperm entering egg.

male then releases sperm over the eggs to fertilise them. The eggs have to be fertilised as soon as they leave the female's cloaca, for the 'jelly' around the eggs swells in the water and stops the sperm entering them.

The sperms of the male are like minute tadpoles. They swim towards the female eggs. Each sperm can fertilise only one egg. As soon as the sperm enters the egg, it begins to develop into a frog.

The natterjack toad, below, eats the same food as the frog and is therefore the frog's rival.

The picture above shows from top to bottom the eggs of the common frog, the common toad and the natterjack toad within the jelly covering.

The first few days

After mating, both the male and female frog leave the eggs and take no further interest in them. The eggs settle at the bottom of the pond until the jelly has swelled with water, when they then float up to the surface. This is shown in the large picture above. The jelly around the eggs absorbs the heat from the sun, thus keeping the eggs warm. It also protects them against fungi and germs. In addition, it enables the eggs to stick together in masses

The stickleback often inhabits the same pool as the frog. Usually of dull colouring, the stickleback changes its colour during the breeding season as we see it here.

known as 'frog-spawn'. The jelly is not used as food. The food comes from the egg inside the jelly. When the egg leaves the cloaca it contains not only the future frog but also yolk upon which it will feed.

Development of an egg starts within two to three hours. The egg and jelly around it at this time measures about 8 to 10 mm across.

Of the thousands of eggs laid by the female frog, a great many are eaten by enemies such as fishes, snakes and water insects.

At first the egg grows and then divides into many 'cells'. Any time after the third day the egg inside the jelly takes on a different shape; it is no longer round but rather more bean-shaped. Two or three days later the egg has a definite tadpole shape. After about ten days the tadpole is longer still and it moves about quite a lot within the jelly. Its tail is finned, and it has developed gills through which it breathes.

Picture 1 shows the underside of the tadpole a few days after hatching. Its suckers have now divided in two and can be seen behind the mouth. It breathes through the external gills on each side of its body. The fold of skin which lies between each set of gills is called the operculum.

Picture 2 shows the underside of the tadpole at the end of the fourth week. The operculum grows over the external gills leaving an opening on the left side of the body called the spiracle. The external gills are then absorbed into the body. The spiral shape in the body is the intestines.

Development of the tadpole
By the end of the second week the tadpole wriggles within the jelly until the jelly punctures and the tadpole escapes. The tadpole clings to the remains of the jelly by means of special sticky 'suckers' as shown, greatly magnified, on this page. It also sticks to water weeds. While the tadpole clings to the jelly mass it is developing all the time. A mouth begins to form in front of the suckers but these suckers will not disappear until the mouth is fully formed. The external gills disappear and internal gills take their place, developing from 'buds' on each side of the head.

1

2

The picture shows many tadpoles clinging to the jelly from which they have just escaped.

3. End of fifth week. The hind legs appear in the form of 'buds'.

4. During the eighth week. The tadpole's hind legs are fully developed and the tadpole has toes.

5. Twelfth week and onwards. The tadpole's forelegs appear. The eyes are larger and have lids. The tadpole now has a new skin.

From tadpole to frog

By the fifth week the tadpole starts to develop the limbs that make it look like a frog and the hind leg buds begin to appear. By this time, too, the tadpole is eating algae. In the seventh week the hind limbs have divided into joints and shortly afterwards the toes appear. Meanwhile, the forelegs are developing underneath the operculum and the tadpole has developed lungs which it can use to gulp air at the surface of the water.

All this time the tadpole has been developing rapidly. Then at about three months the greatest changes of all occur. The tadpole completely changes its form. This change is known as metamorphosis (pronounced met-a-more-fō-sis). The tadpole stops feeding and casts its skin. Its true mouth becomes much wider. The gills disappear and the eyes become larger and develop lids. The forelimbs appear. The stomach becomes less rounded. Many changes are also happening inside the tadpole.

At this time the tail of the tadpole weighs as

6. The tail shortens as the tadpole absorbs its substances into the body as a food.

7. The tadpole is looking more like a frog. Its tail has almost disappeared. It can now move through the water by paddling with its hind legs.

8. The tail has completely disappeared and the tadpole is now a young frog.

much as one-third of its total weight. Its long tail plays a vital part in the future developments that take place. The tadpole digests and absorbs the substance of the tail into its body. This supplies it with the food it needs while so many great changes take place.

The young frog
The young frog or froglet, as he is sometimes called, is ready to leave the water about three months after hatching. Its body is now about 12 mm long and its prime concern is to eat and grow as much as it can before the winter hibernation. By then the frog will have reached a length of 20 mm. At first it catches tiny insects, and in the picture overleaf, a froglet, greatly magnified, is about to catch a greenfly. It will be some time before it is big enough to catch the slugs, snails, beetles, flies and other large insects that adult frogs live on.

A frog is not mature until it is three years of age. Then it can mate and produce more frogs.

| The adult frog flicks its tongue towards its prey, a fly. | The fly is trapped on the sticky end of the frog's tongue. | The frog rolls up its tongue and takes the fly to the back of its throat. |

The frog's tongue
Frogs catch their food with their tongues. A frog's tongue is special because it is fixed to the front of the mouth at the lower jaw and not at the back like a human's tongue. The frog's tongue is thick and flat; it is forked at the front and very elastic. The frog catches insects by flicking the tongue out at great speed. The insect is trapped on the sticky end of the tongue. The frog then rolls up its tongue and takes the fly to the back of its throat.

The frog's eyes
The frog's eyes are placed high on its head to enable it to see while its body is partly submerged in water. It has a fleshy eye-lid at the top and bottom of each eye. In addition it has a third transparent eye-lid which moves upwards to give protection to the eyeball when the frog is in the water or to keep the eyeball moist when on land. The eyes also help in swallowing food. The eyeballs can be pulled down into the roof of the mouth to squash

The transparent layer of skin the frog sheds first splits down the middle of the back. The frog then uses his limbs to get rid of the skin.

It takes an hour or more for the frog to shed a layer of skin which the frog then eats.

The frog's eyes are placed high on its head enabling it to peer over the top of the water.

insects. Then the fleshy lids close.

The frog's skin
The skin of the frog plays a most important function in its survival. Although the frog has lungs and breathes through its nostrils, the intake of air by this means is still not enough to enable the frog to live comfortably on land. The frog therefore takes in a vast amount of air through the skin. In fact, during the period of underwater hibernation the frog does not breathe through its lungs at all but relies entirely on its skin.

The skin also absorbs water, as the frog does not drink. Glands on the skin help keep the skin moist whilst the frog is out of water. The frog renews its skin every month or so during the summer, and the skin shedding process is shown in the top picture above. Another function of the skin is to change its colour to blend with the surroundings and make it difficult for its enemies to see it.

Left: a grass snake swallowing the common frog.

Below: the male Mallard duck hunts the frog in the water.

Predators

Frogs have many enemies and these are called predators. In the water the frog's enemies include water beetles, many species of fish, birds such as the duck, stork and heron, and mammals such as the otter. On land, frogs are eaten mainly by grass snakes, which will even enter the water to catch them. They are also eaten by birds, hedgehogs, foxes and badgers. In fact, the list is almost endless. Man is also one of the frog's greatest enemies. He will catch the edible frog to eat and other frogs for use as bait. More important, he destroys the frogs' breeding ponds by polluting the water and draining the land.

The frog has few defences against its enemies. Although it can jump very well, compared with most of its enemies, the frog moves slowly and is therefore unable to avoid attack. However, it does have one or two

The red fox of Europe looking at a common frog in its defence posture.

The large fast-moving pike has little difficulty in catching a frog in water.

defences. In some species of frog, the skin secretes a poison with a burning taste. The common frog takes up a defence posture by covering its eyes with its fore limbs and drawing in the hind legs against its body which it has puffed out. This posture would perhaps make it more difficult for the frog to be gripped by a predator. Some frogs have skins of a similar colour to their surroundings and are therefore camouflaged.

Its ability to live both in the water and on the land offers some sort of protection since the frog on land can evade a land predator by hopping into the water. Likewise he can escape fishes by moving out of the water on to the land.

Out of the 2,000 eggs (1) that a female frog can lay, it is possible for as few as 50 to survive (2) and turn into tadpoles (3).

Despite the many dangers throughout its entire life cycle, enough frogs live to carry on breeding (4).

The amount of light available plays an important part in a frog's camouflage. On 'light' days the frog's colour lightens and on 'darker' days the frog's colour darkens, thus enabling it to blend in with the background. Other factors such as heat, dryness, moisture and darkness also affect the frog's colour.

The common bullfrog of North America is shown here with a bullfrog tadpole. The tadpole grows to a length of between 16 and 18 cm. This species of frog appears very late from its winter sleep, sometimes as late as July, and its tadpoles therefore, have to hibernate in the first winter of life.

The largest and smallest
The largest frog is the goliath frog of West Africa. The smallest is the arrow-poison frog of Cuba. A goliath frog found in 1960 was recorded as measuring 34 cm from snout to vent while the arrow-poison frog measures only 8 to 12 mm. The common frog is the largest native British frog, measuring from 4 cm to 9.5 cm.

The picture above shows, from top to bottom, the goliath frog, which has been drawn to just over half its true size; the common frog and the tiny arrow-poison frog.

1. The arrow-poison frog of Central and South America.

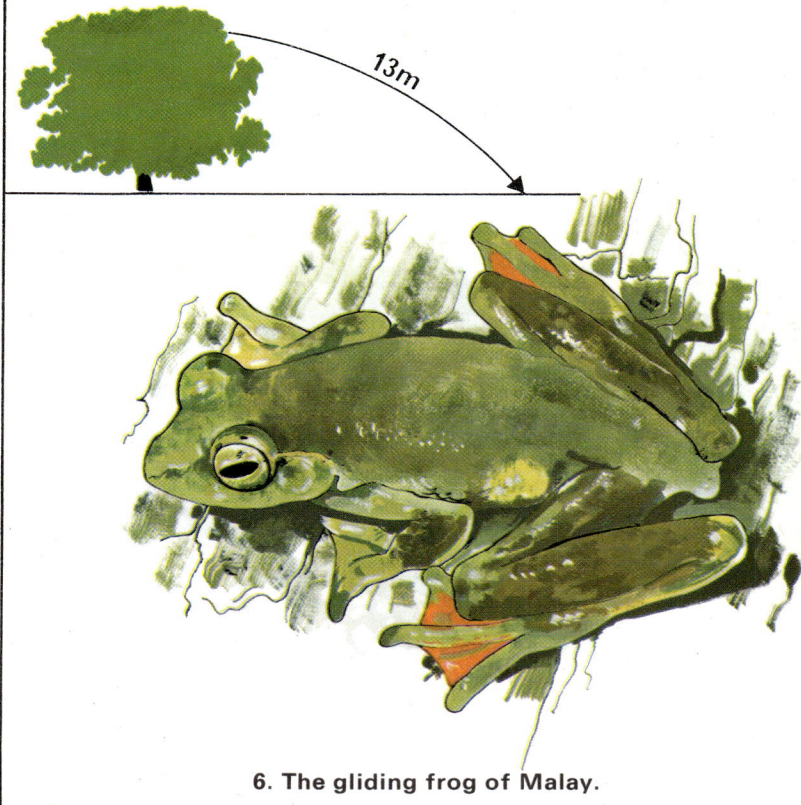

2. The hairy frog of West Africa.

5. The painted reed frog of Africa.

6. The gliding frog of Malay.

1. The arrow-poison frog is one of the few frogs which secrete a poison strong enough to kill. South American Indians used the poison to tip their arrow heads. The frog is very brightly coloured and these colours warn other animals that they are unfit to eat.

2. The hairy frog's 'hairs' are really extra gills that the male frog develops during the breeding season. It is possible that the 'hairs' help to tell other males not to breed with it, for it often happens that males of other species will try to mate with other males. Male hairy frogs spend most of their time in the water but the females stay on land except in the breeding season.

3. Unlike most species of frog, the leaf or horned frog is a ferocious creature and is cannibalistic—which means that it will eat its own kind. It is a large amphibian and measures up to 25 cm. The horned frogs of South America and Asia are not related in any way although they are similar in appearance and have similar characteristics. As the picture shows, this frog looks remarkably like a leaf.

4. The leopard frog is the most common frog in North America. The size of the male averages 9 cm while the female is slightly larger. It is abundant in Florida and is eaten as a delicacy in Texas. The leopard frog travels

3. The leaf frog of South-east Asia.

4. The leopard frog of North America.

7. The clawed frog of Southern Africa.

8. The tree frog of East Africa.

considerable distances from its pond.

5. There are more than 200 species of reed frogs living in Africa. Most of them are beautifully colourful and patterned as the painted reed frog seen in the picture shows. These frogs, although colourful, are sometimes difficult to identify, as their colouring varies so much from region to region.

6. The gliding frog of Malay belongs to the family of tree frogs. Unlike most other frogs which breed in water, the gliding frog makes a foam nest among large tree leaves. They are most active at night when they take gliding leaps from tree to tree. Some gliding frogs are able to cover a distance of 15 metres to the base of a tree.

7. The clawed frog is very much a water frog and will only leave the water when drought forces it to find other water holes. It has strong back legs and large webbed hind feet. It is a strong swimmer but is extremely clumsy on land. This frog can change its colour to suit its surroundings.

8. Like most other tree frogs, the tree frog of East Africa spends most of its life in trees. Because of this, on the toes of fore and hind feet of all tree frogs, there are special suckers whicn enable the frog to cling to branches.

The male frog mates with the female.
He releases his sperm . . .
which fertilises her eggs . . .
that swell into frog-spawn . . .
that grow into tadpoles . . .
that change into froglets . . .
that grow to adults that mate . . .